GO FACTS Physical science

Energy

A & C BLACK • LONDON

Energy

© 2007 Blake Publishing
Additional Material © A & C Black Publishers Ltd 2008

First published in 2007 in Australia by Blake Education Pty Ltd.

This edition published 2008 in the United Kingdom by
A & C Black Publishers Ltd, 38 Soho Square, London W1D 3HB.

Hardback edition
ISBN 9781408102626

Paperback edition
ISBN 9781408104873

A CIP record for this book is available from the British Library.

Author: Ian Rohr
Publishers: Katy Pike
Editor: Mark Stafford
Design and layout by The Modern Art Production Group

Image credits: p4 (top), p13 (top)–NASA JPL; p5 (bottom left)–NASA NSSDC,
courtesy of the Extreme–Ultraviolet Imaging Telescope Consortium;
p10-11 (all)–Mark Stafford; p17 (top)–US Navy photo by Photographer's Mate
Airman Rob Gaston; p17 (bottom left)–NASA; p18 (bottom) Shutterstock.

Printed in China by WKT Company Ltd.

This book is produced using paper that is made from wood grown in
managed sustainable forests. It is natural, renewable and recyclable.
The logging and manufacturing processes conform to the environmental
regulations of the country of origin.

contents

What is Energy?

Energy is the ability to do **work**. It makes things happen.

There are different forms of energy, such as electrical and light energy. Energy cannot be created or destroyed. But it is always moving and changing form.

When you rub your hands together, you use energy stored in your body to make your hands move. Your hands heat up. This is some of your energy changing into heat.

Almost all our energy comes from the Sun. Plants use light energy to make food, which people and animals eat. Light and heat energy make the air move as wind. Millions of years ago, energy from the Sun grew the plants and animals that became the **fossil fuels** we burn today.

Electricity is made in power stations. It would take 1.7 billion power stations to produce the same amount of energy coming to the Earth from the Sun. That is roughly one power station for every four people on the planet.

DID YOU KNOW?

Energy is measured in units called joules.
How much energy is needed for these actions?

Action	Number of joules needed
To lift a small apple one metre from the ground	1
To raise the temperature of one litre of water by one degree Celsius	4,186
To power an average light bulb for one hour	216,000

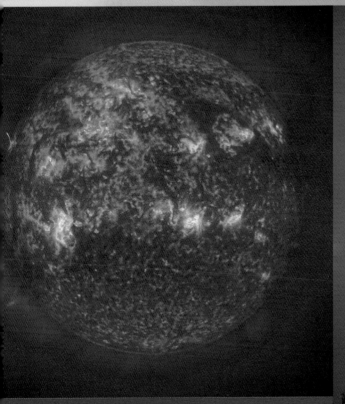

Two-thirds of the world's electricity comes from burning fossil fuels in power stations, like this one.

Our Sun is about 4.6 billion years old.

5

Thermal Energy

Thermal energy moves between objects that have different temperatures. When thermal energy moves it is called heat.

Thermal energy always moves to something cooler. This is why you lose heat from your body on a cold day.

When thermal energy moves through a solid, such as a spoon, it is called conduction. When it moves through a liquid, such as a hot drink, it is called convection. When it moves through space, it is called radiation.

Our planet stores a huge amount of thermal energy. The world's oceans absorb heat from the Sun. Heat energy inside the Earth is called **geothermal** energy. Some of this energy comes to the surface as hot water. Geothermal energy is used for heating and to make electricity.

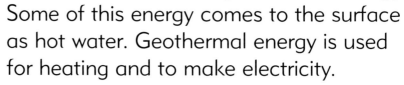
Ice is stored thermal energy.

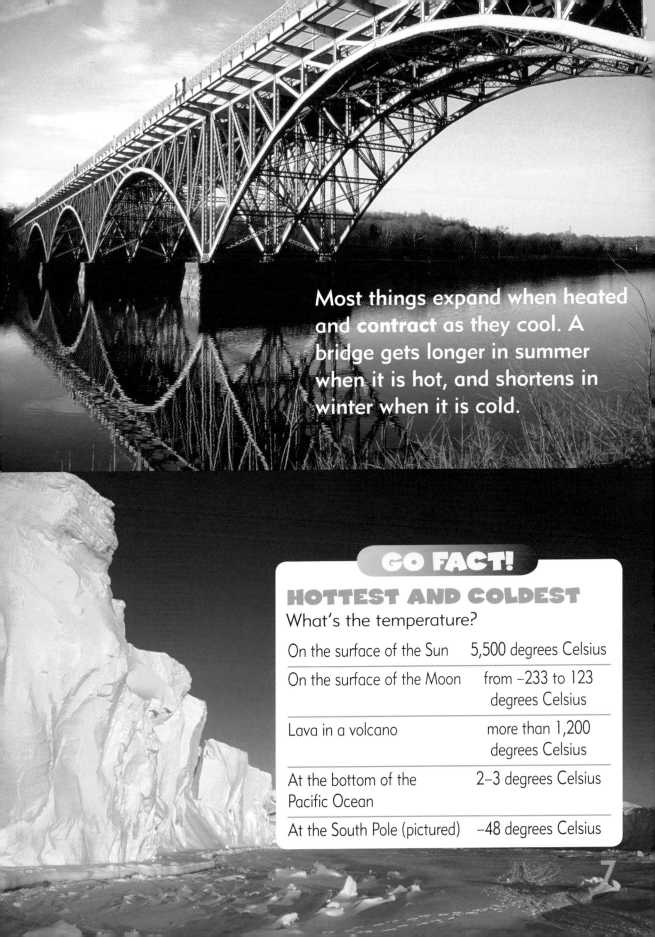

Most things expand when heated and **contract** as they cool. A bridge gets longer in summer when it is hot, and shortens in winter when it is cold.

GO FACT!

HOTTEST AND COLDEST

What's the temperature?

On the surface of the Sun	5,500 degrees Celsius
On the surface of the Moon	from −233 to 123 degrees Celsius
Lava in a volcano	more than 1,200 degrees Celsius
At the bottom of the Pacific Ocean	2–3 degrees Celsius
At the South Pole (pictured)	−48 degrees Celsius

7

Electrical Energy

Electrical energy is work done by electricity.

A light bulb converts electricity into light and heat.

Electricity is the movement or presence of an **electrical charge**. A moving electrical charge is called a **current**.

The most common way to make electricity is to burn a fuel, such as coal. This heats water to make steam. The steam spins a **turbine**. This powers a **generator** to make electricity.

There are other ways to make electricity. Wind and water can also power a generator. A **solar cell** absorbs sunlight to make electricity.

Electrical energy can be **converted** into other forms of energy, such as heat, light and sound.

Static electricity is an electrical charge that builds up on objects when they rub against each other. It can even build up on you. You may get a small electrical shock from touching something made of metal, such as a door knob or car. The electricity jumps between you and the metal.

Lightning is an electrical current that jumps through the air. The current heats the air hotter than the surface of the Sun. This causes a flash. The air expands and vibrates, making a sound that we hear as thunder.

GO FACT!

THE MOST

Central Africa receives more lightning strikes than any other place on Earth.

Make Your Own Lightning

Follow these steps to make miniature lightning.

Do this experiment on a dry day. If the air is damp, the experiment might not work.

What you need:

- an inflated balloon
- wool clothing, such as a jumper
- a metal surface, such as a door knob or filing cabinet

1 Darken the room as much as possible. A dark room will help you see the spark.

2 Rub the balloon quickly against the wool. Do this 10 to 15 times. Rubbing the balloon builds up static electricity.

3 Move the balloon close to the metal surface. The spark that jumps between the balloon and the metal surface is like lightning, just on a smaller scale.

Light and Sound Energy

Everything we see and hear is light and sound energy.

Light moves through space at 300,000 kilometres per second. It is the fastest thing in the universe. Light slows down when it moves through air, water and glass.

Sound energy moves much more slowly – about 340 metres per second. A thunderstorm shows the difference in speed between light and sound. Lightning causes thunder, but you see lightning before you hear thunder because light moves faster than sound.

Sound energy moves in a wave. It is released by vibrations, such as when a guitar is strummed. Fast vibrations make higher-pitched sounds, and slow vibrations make lower-pitched sounds.

The vocal cords in your throat vibrate to make sounds. You can feel the vibrations if you put your fingers lightly on your throat while you speak.

DID YOU KNOW?

How long does light take to reach the Earth?

Light from:	Time:
The Sun	8.3 minutes
A star called Proxima Centauri	4.3 years
A galaxy called Andromeda (pictured)	2.3 million years

Whales use sound to communicate. Sound travels almost five times faster in water than through air.

Chemical Energy

Chemical energy is stored in the bonds between **atoms**. Bonds are the forces that link atoms.

Chemical energy can be stored. There is chemical energy stored in the tip of a match. When the match is struck and burns, the energy is released as heat and light.

Chemical energy is also stored in natural gas. If natural gas is burned in a heater, its chemical energy is converted into heat and light energy. If natural gas is burned inside the engine of a bus, some of the chemical energy is used to make the bus move.

A plant changes light energy into chemical energy. It stores the chemical energy. This process is called **photosynthesis**. When an animal eats the plant, it absorbs the energy.

Fruit contains stored chemical energy!

The chemical energy in batteries is converted into electrical energy.

The chemical energy in a firework becomes light, heat and sound energy.

When you run, the muscles in your legs provide the moving force, but chemical energy powers your muscles.

GO FACT!

THE LARGEST
The world's largest firework was used at the Lake Toya Firework Festival in Japan in 1988. It weighed 700 kilograms and produced an explosion 1.2 kilometres wide.

Nuclear Energy

Nuclear energy is the energy stored inside an atom.

Atoms are very small pieces of matter. One hundred million atoms in a line would only be one centimetre long. Nuclear energy is released when the bonds inside an atom are formed or broken. This is called a nuclear reaction.

A nuclear reaction can be controlled. This happens inside a nuclear power station. The energy released from the reaction is used to make electricity. One kilogram of uranium produces as much energy as about 20,000 kilograms of coal.

A nuclear reaction may also be uncontrolled and occur very quickly – in less than a second. This releases a huge amount of heat and light energy. This is how nuclear weapons work.

Nuclear energy is also used in medicine. It can be used to see inside patients and treat people with cancer.

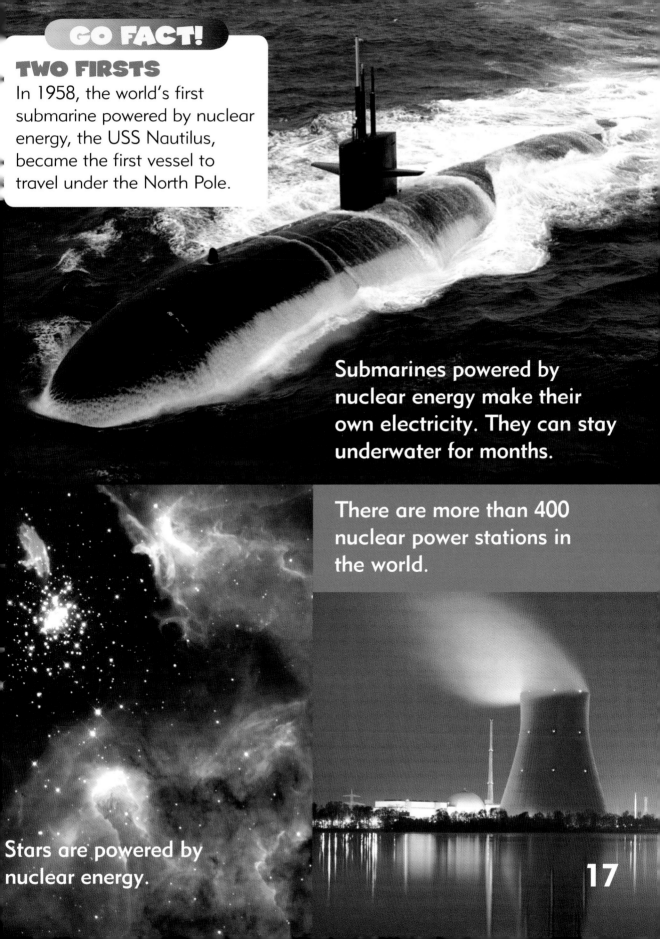

TWO FIRSTS

In 1958, the world's first submarine powered by nuclear energy, the USS Nautilus, became the first vessel to travel under the North Pole.

Submarines powered by nuclear energy make their own electricity. They can stay underwater for months.

There are more than 400 nuclear power stations in the world.

Stars are powered by nuclear energy.

17

Potential and Kinetic

Work waiting to be done is potential energy. Work being done is kinetic energy.

Potential energy is energy that could be released or used. A coiled spring has potential energy because the spring could uncoil. A rock on the edge of a cliff has potential energy. Its potential energy is the energy that would be released if it fell from the cliff.

The food we eat becomes potential energy when it is stored in our bodies. When this energy is used to do things, such as kick a ball, it becomes kinetic energy.

Kinetic energy is the energy of movement. It is the energy something has because it is moving. When the spring uncoils or the rock falls, the energy changes from potential to kinetic.

The more something weighs and the faster it moves, the more kinetic energy it has.

Batteries have potential energy.

18

At the top of the loop, the roller coaster car's energy is mainly potential energy.

As it gets faster, the roller coaster car's energy is mainly kinetic energy.

There is potential energy in a stretched rubber band.

Converting Energy

The potential energy of stored water can be converted into other forms of energy.

Water stored in dams can be used to generate electricity. This type of electricity is called **hydroelectricity**. 'Hydro' means 'water'.

1. Water stored in a dam has potential energy.

2. When the water is released, its kinetic energy turns turbines to power a generator.

3. The generator produces electricity.

4. Electricity is converted into thermal, light and sound energy.

GO FACT!
DID YOU KNOW?
About two per cent of the UK's electricity is hydroelectricity, compared to about 99 per cent of Norway's electricity.

Energy Sources

Energy sources that will never run out are called renewable.

Energy source		Is it renewable?
Solar		yes
Wind		yes
Oil		no
Coal		no
Nuclear		no

Glossary

atom	a very small piece of matter
chemical	relating to chemicals; chemicals are substances that react to each other
contract	to become shorter or narrower
converted	changed into something else
current	a movement of water, air or electrical charge
electrical charge	a basic property of matter; it can be positive, negative or neutral (no electrical charge)
fossil fuel	fuels formed from plants and animals that died millions of years ago
generator	a machine that converts kinetic energy into electricity
geothermal	relating to heat inside the Earth
hydroelectricity	electricity made from the energy of falling water
photosynthesis	how plants convert light energy into chemical energy
solar cell	a device that converts light energy directly into electricity
turbine	a machine that turns when liquid or gas flows through it
work	a transfer of energy to make something move

Index

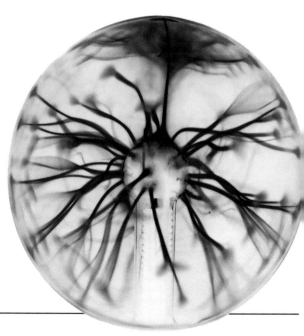